ANSWERS
Essential Music Theory
Levels 1-3

San Marco Publications

Mark Sarnecki

Elementary Music Theory © 2024 by San Marco Publications. All rights reserved.

All right reserved. No part of this book may be reproduced in any form or by electronic or mechanical means including Information storage and retrieval systems without permission in writing from the author.

ISNB: 9781896499482

Level 1-3 Answers

Page 8, No. 1

F D B A E E
G F C A B D
E D C B A G
F E A F C D

Page 10, No. 1

B G E D A A
G F C A B D
A G F E D C
A G C A E F

Page 12, No. 1

B C A G B C
B C B D D E
D A F B D C
C D E D E C
A D B B F G

Page 13, No. 2

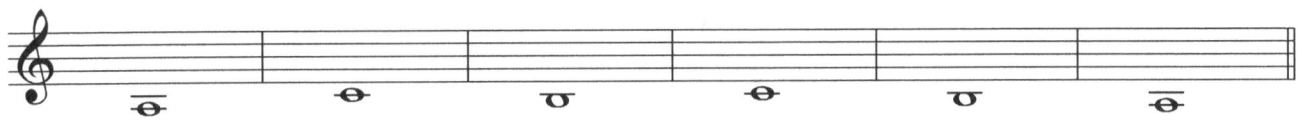

Page 13, No. 3

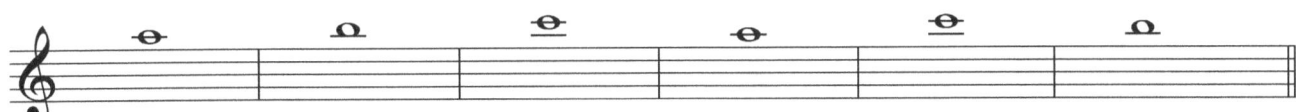

Page 13, No. 4

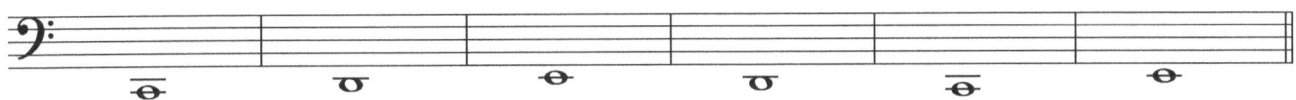

Page 13, No. 5

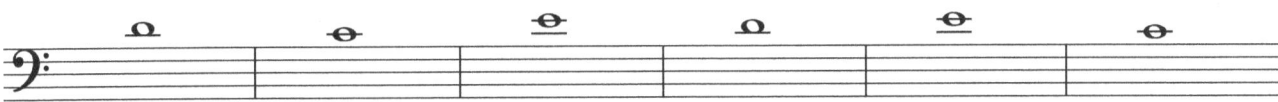

Page 13, No. 6

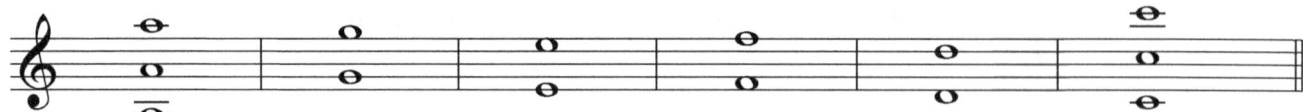

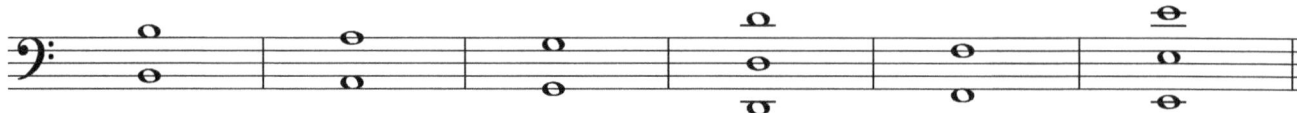

Page 14, No. 1

F C F B A D E C
E D B F G A C C

Page 14, No. 2

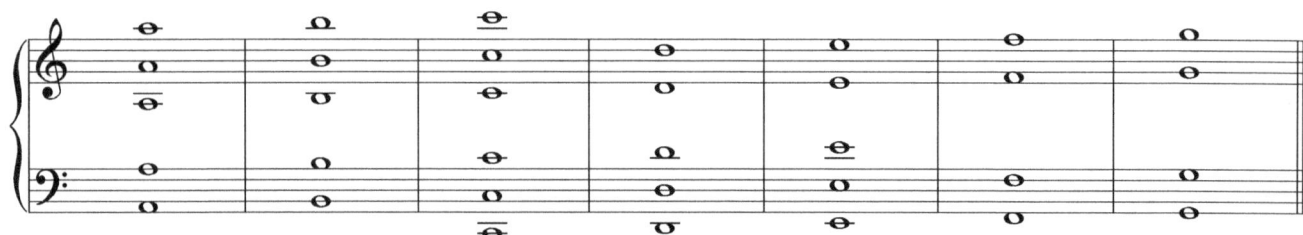

Page 15, No. 3

C B F E D A
B G D C F E

Page 16, other choices are possible

Page 21, No. 1

quarter	eighth
half	eighth
whole	dotted half

Page 21, No. 2

1	1
2	4
1/2	3

Page 22, No. 3

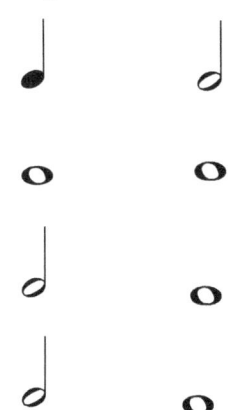

Page 23, No. 1

Page 24, No. 1

Page 27, No. 5

quarter note	eighth rest
half rest	whole rest
whole note	eighth note
quarter rest	half note

Page 28, No. 6

Page 28, No. 7

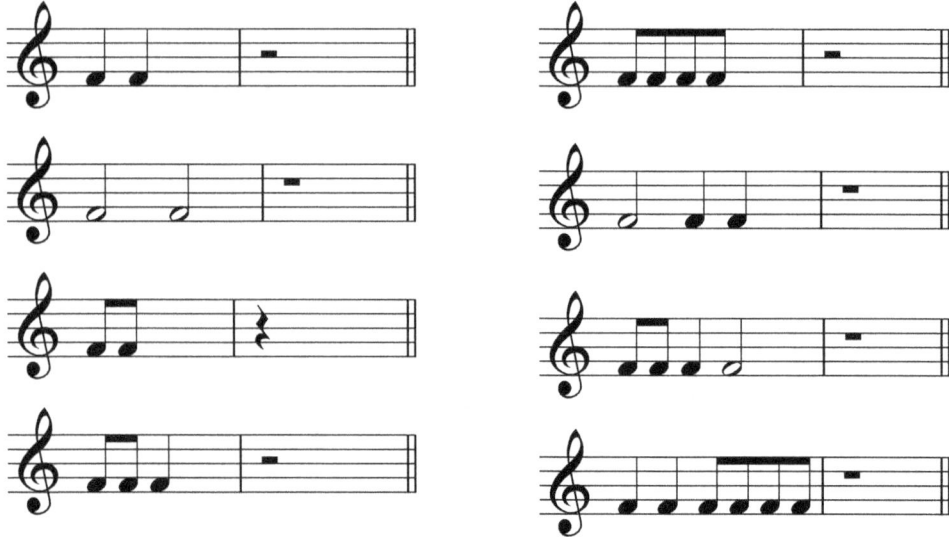

Page 32, No. 1

Page 33, No. 1

Page 34, No. 2

2/4, 4/4, 2/4, 4/4, 3/4

Page 34, No. 3

Page 35, No. 4

Page 35, No. 5

Page 37, No. 1

Page 39, No. 1

Page 40, No. 2

Page 41, No. 1

Page 41, No. 2

Page 43, No. 1

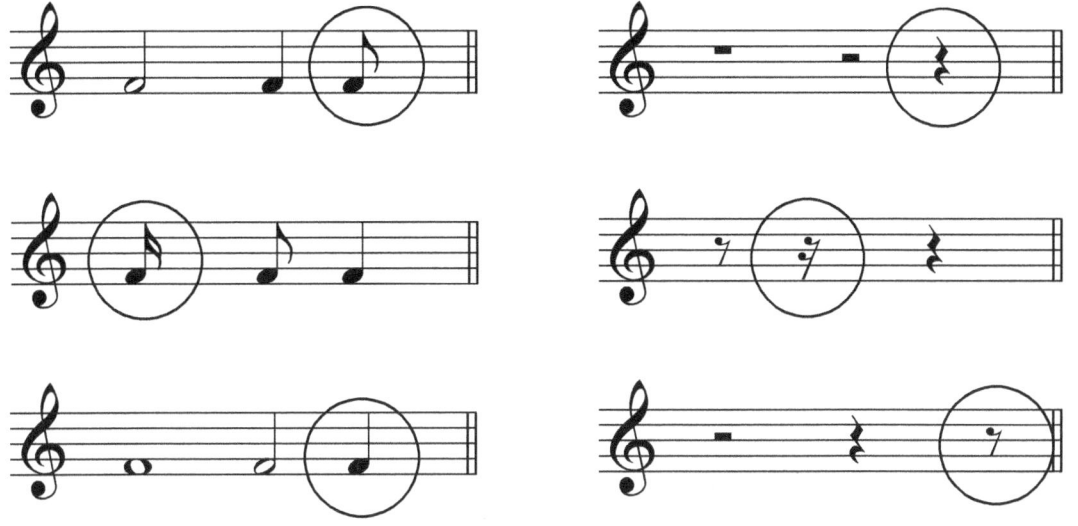

Page 43, No. 2

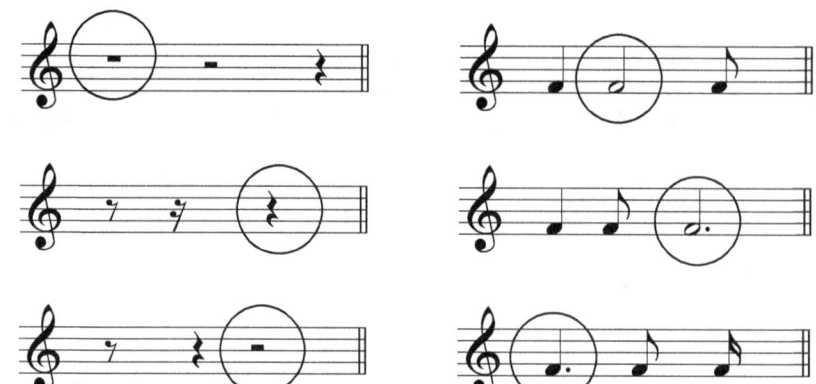

Page 44, No. 1

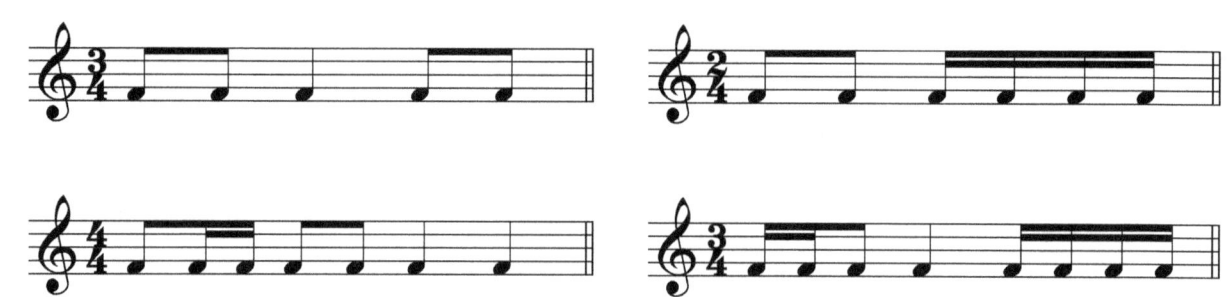

Page 45, No. 2

a) 2   b) 2   c) 2   d) 4   e) 2

Page 45, No. 3

Page 46, No. 4

3/4	3/4
2/4	2/4
4/4	4/4
3/4	4/4
2/4	3/4

Page 46, No. 5

Page48, No. 1

Page 49, No. 2

Bach
English Suite No.2

Corelli
Concerto Grosso
Op. 6, No. 11

Mozart
Sonata in G

Liszt
Hungarian Rhapsody No. 14

Tchaikovsky
Swan Lake

Mozart
Trio in C

Bach
Brandenberg Concerto No. 2

Page 51, No. 1

Allegretto

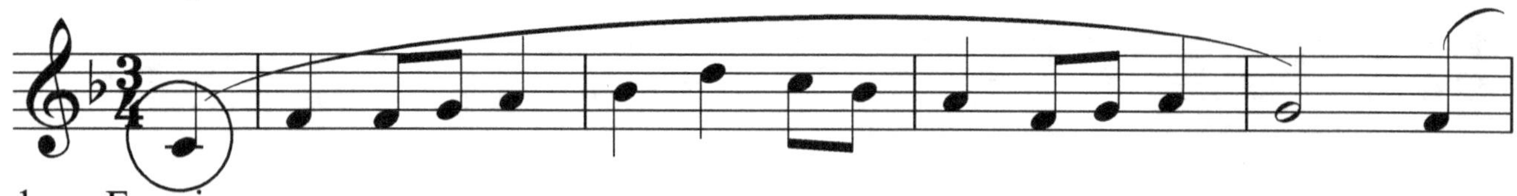

key: F major

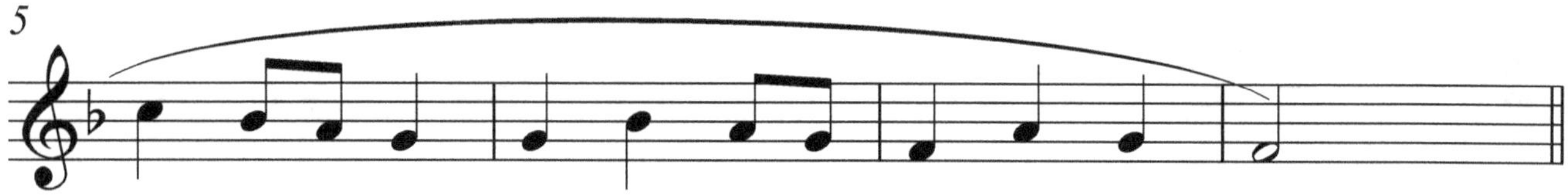

Allegro

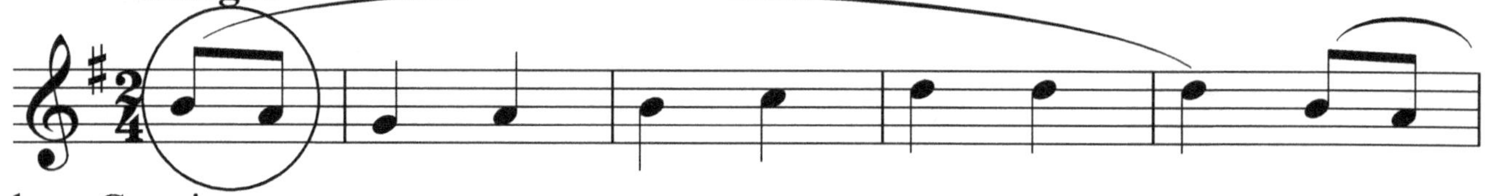

key: G major

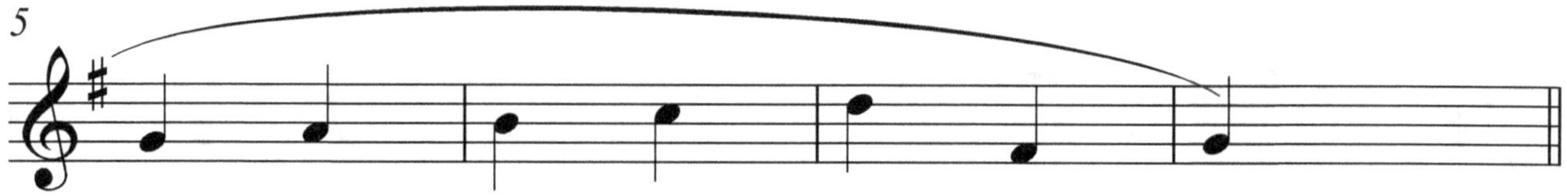

Page 54, No. 1

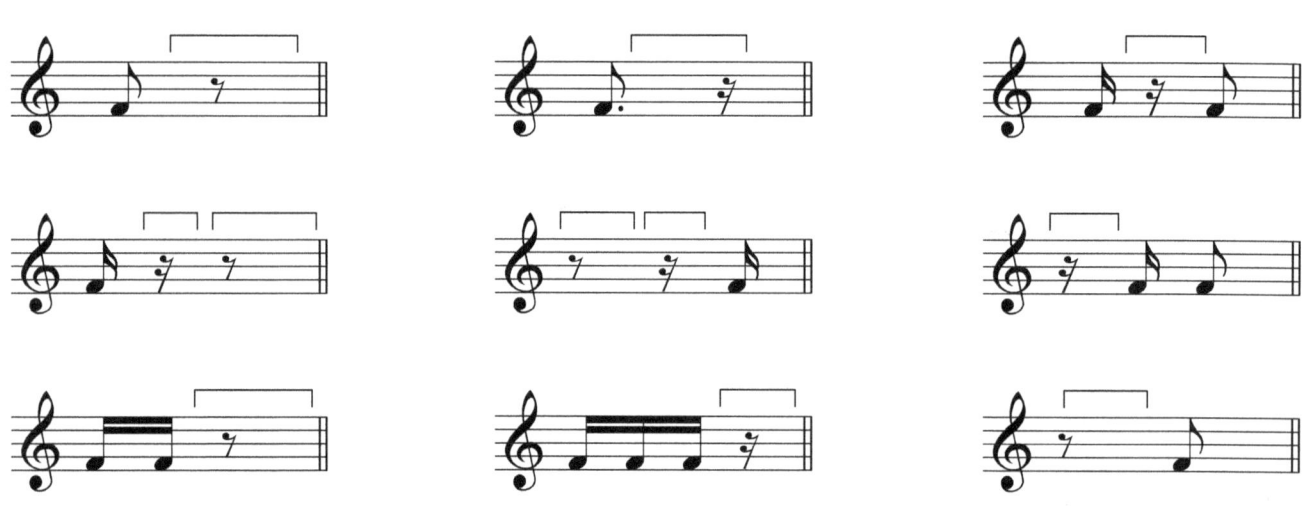

Page 54, No. 2

Page 55, No. 3

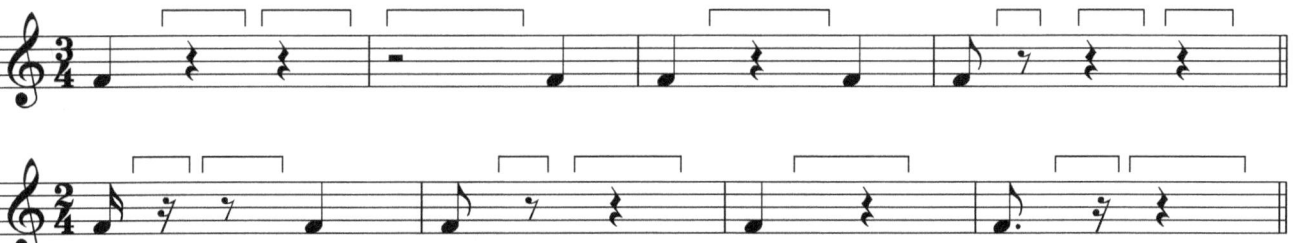

Page 55, No. 4

Page 59, No. 1, other answers are possible

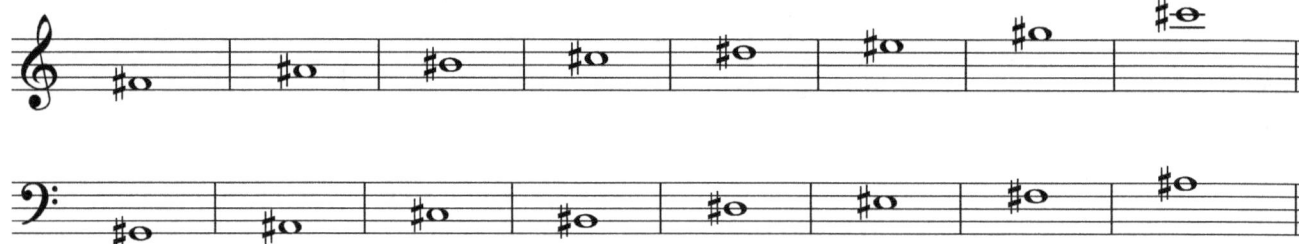

Page 60, No. 2, other answers are possible

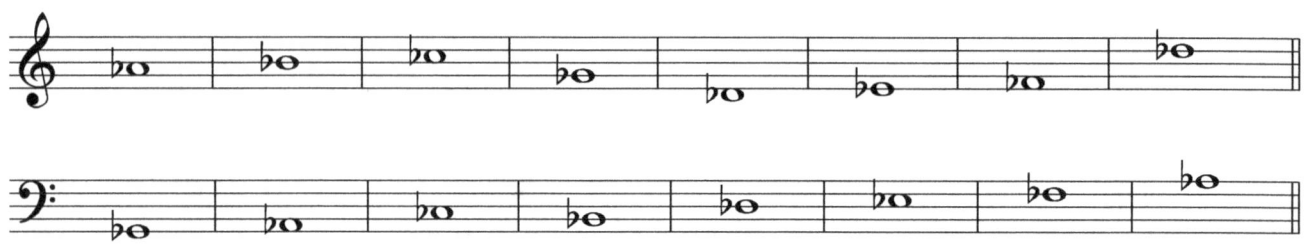

Page 62, No. 3, other answers are possible

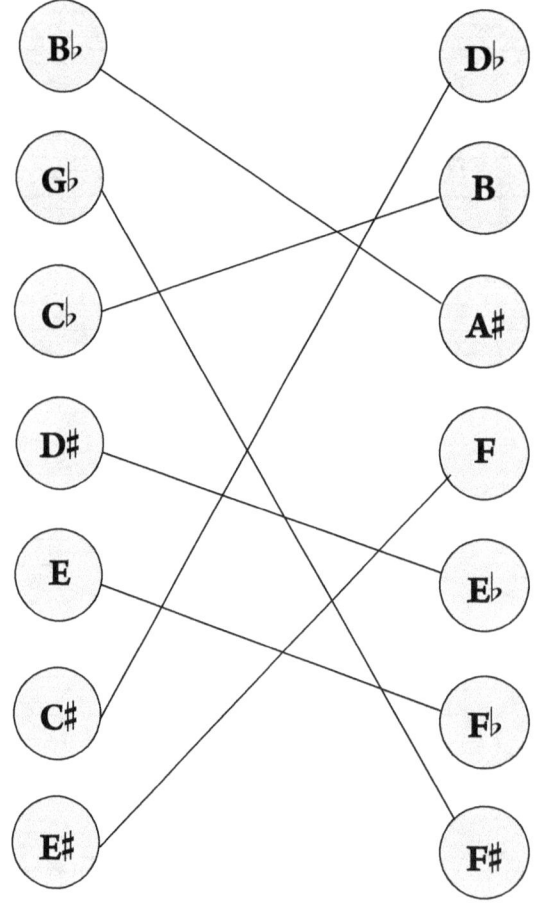

Page 64, No. 1

F# E F# C# D A B♭ E♭ E F# E D

A♭ C E♭ A G# E G B B♭ D B♭ F#

Page 64, No. 2, other options are possible

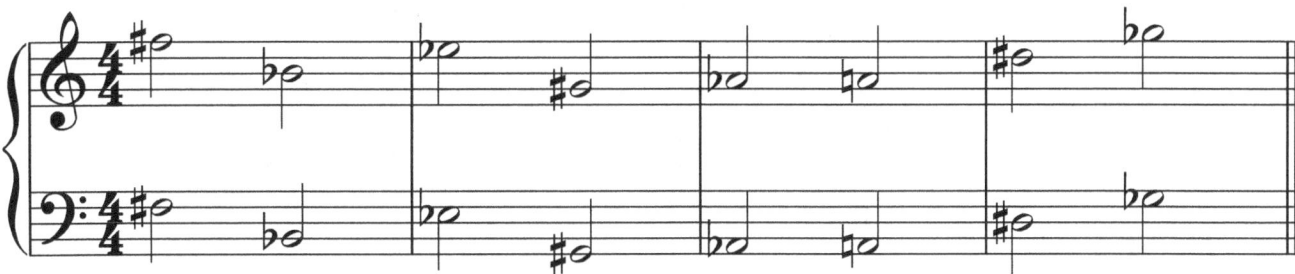

Page 64, No. 3, other options are possible

Page 65, No. 4

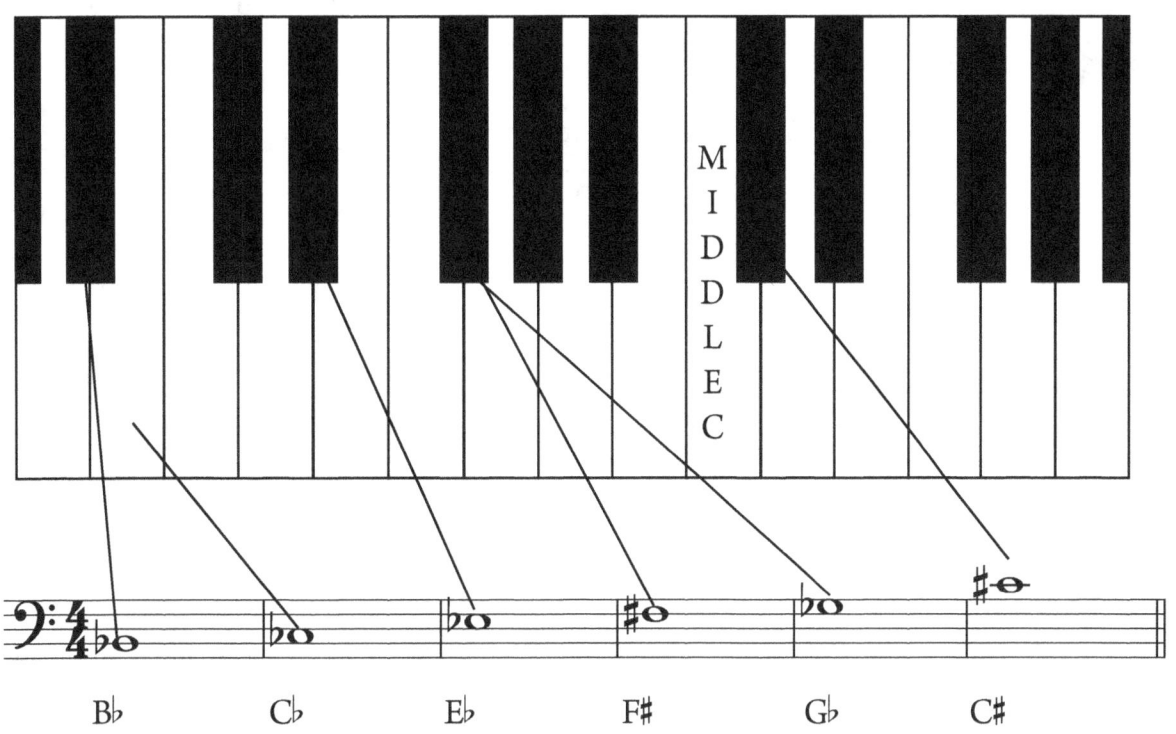

19

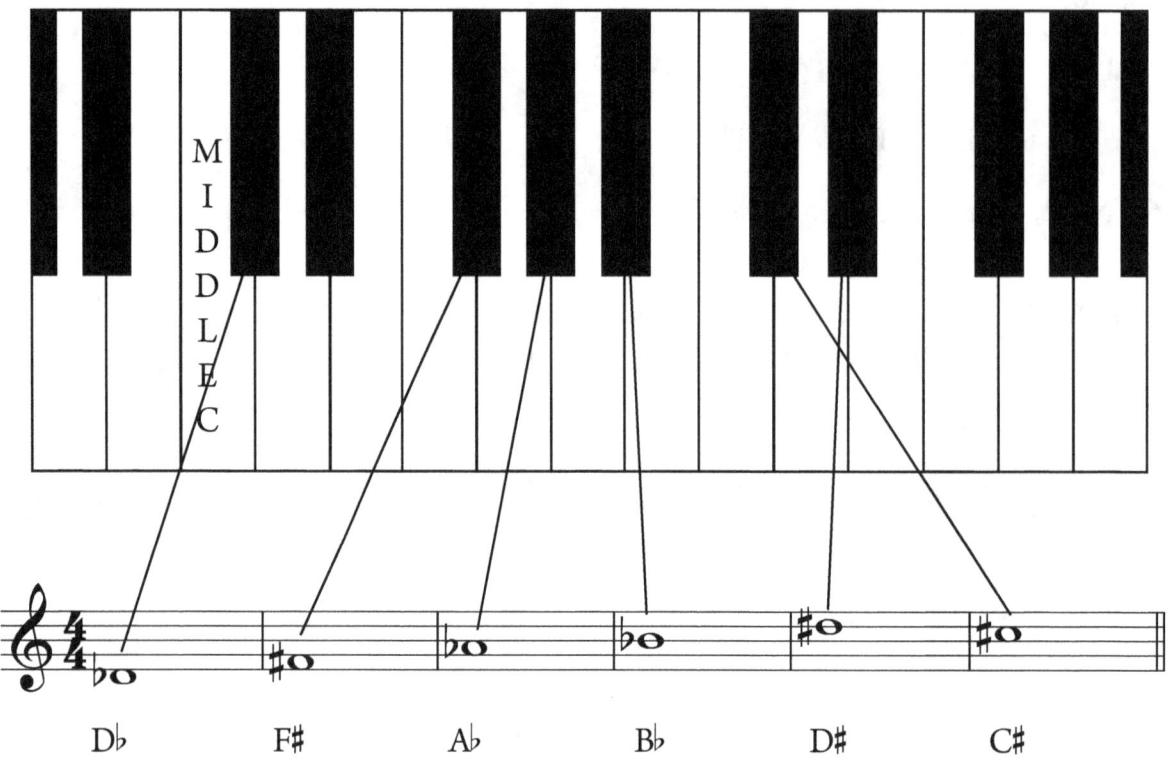

Page 66, No. 5

A whole step	A half step	A whole step	A whole step
A half step	A half step	A half step	A whole step
A whole step	A half step	A half step	A whole step
A half step	A whole step	A half step	A half step

Page 66, No. 6 (other options are possible)

Page 67, No. 7 (other options are possible)

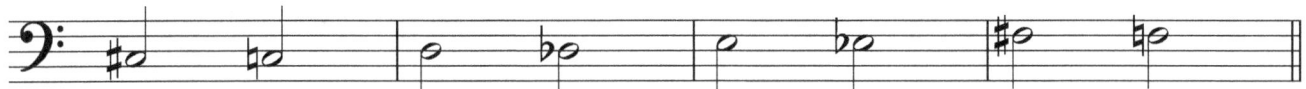

Page 67, No. 8

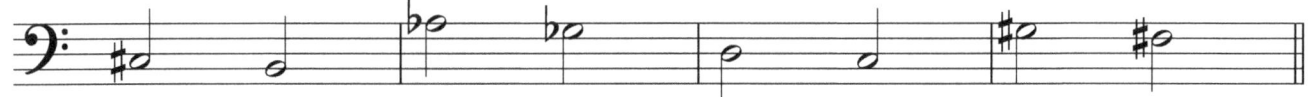

Page 67, No. 9

Page 68, No. 1

Page 68, No. 2

Page 70, No. 1

Page 70, No. 2

Page 70, No. 3

Page 72, No. 1

5 7 2 1 3 7 3 8

4 2 8 6 5 6 2 1

1 8 2 3 6 6 4 5

8 5 2 1 8 3 8 7

Page 73, No. 2

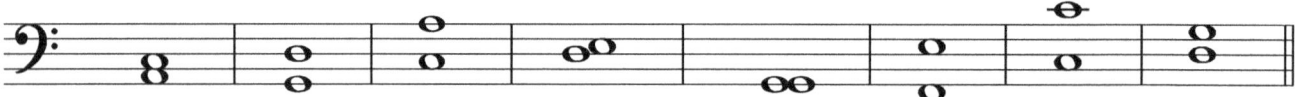

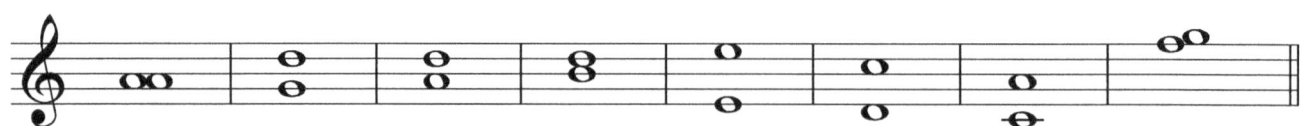

Page 74, No. 3

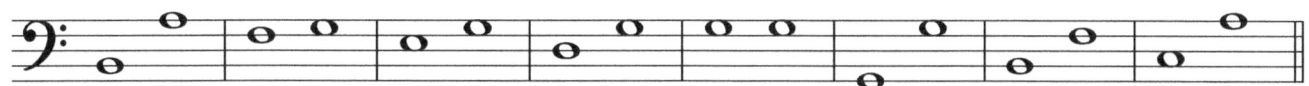

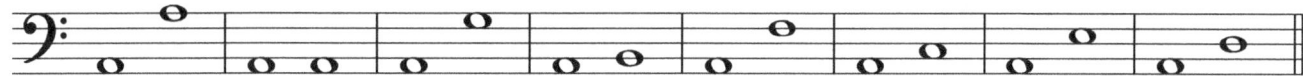

Page 76, No. 1

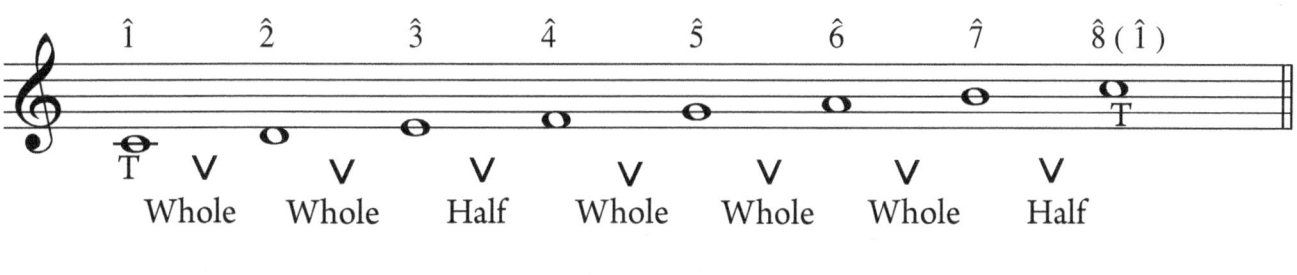

Page 77, No. 2

Page 77, No. 3

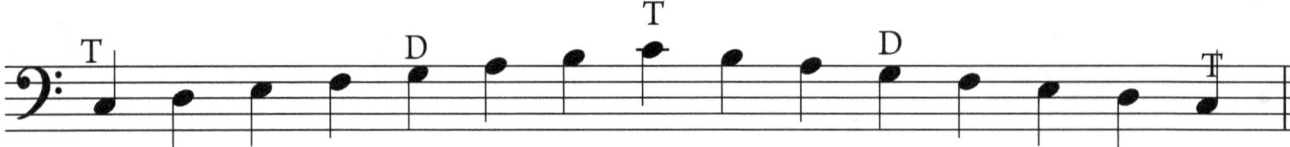

Page 78, No. 4

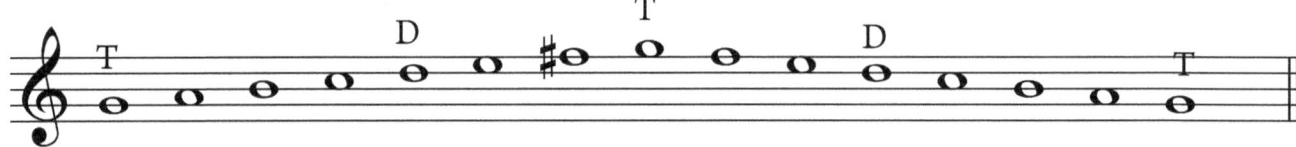

Page 79, No. 5

Page 80, No. 6

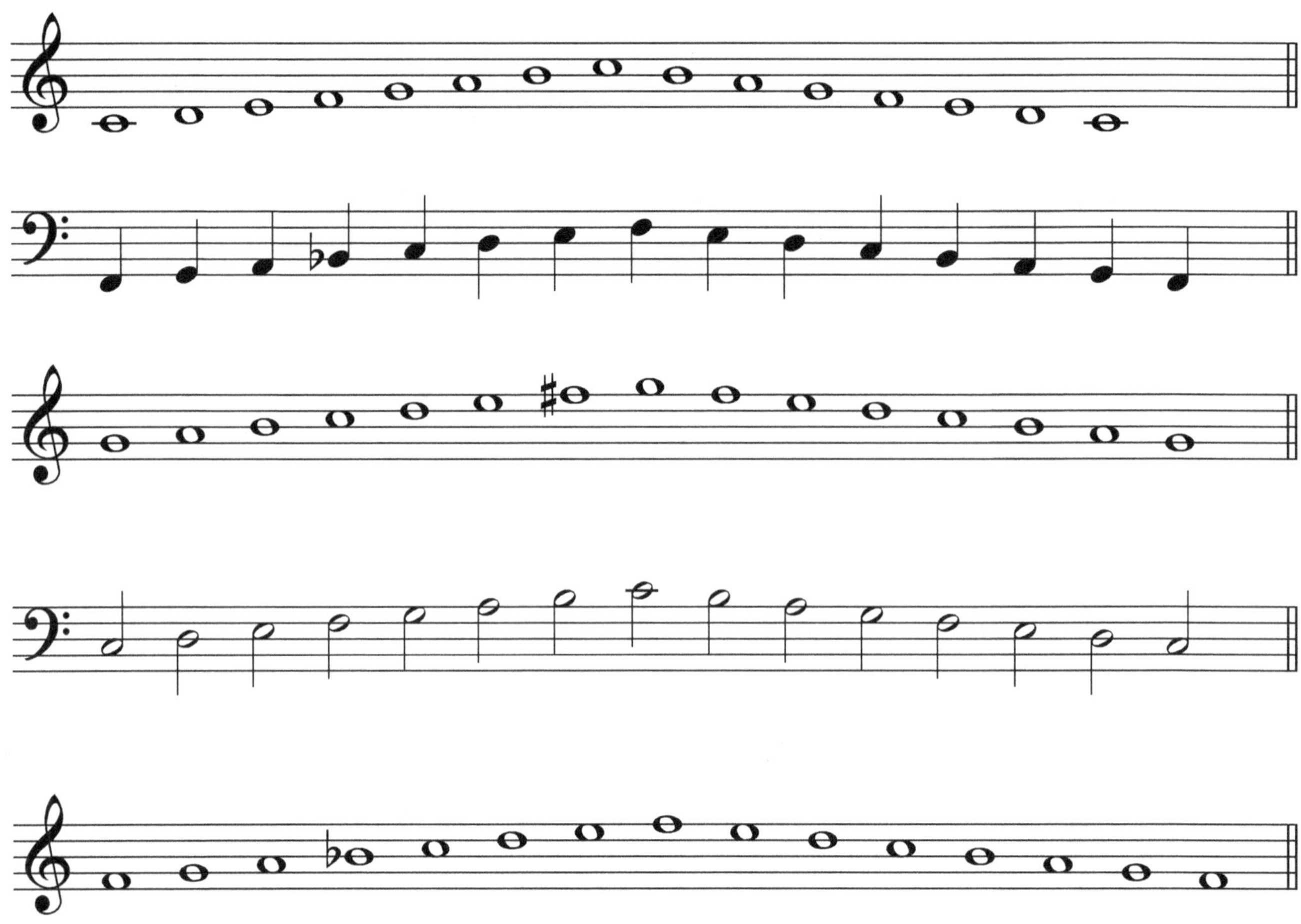

Page 81, No. 7

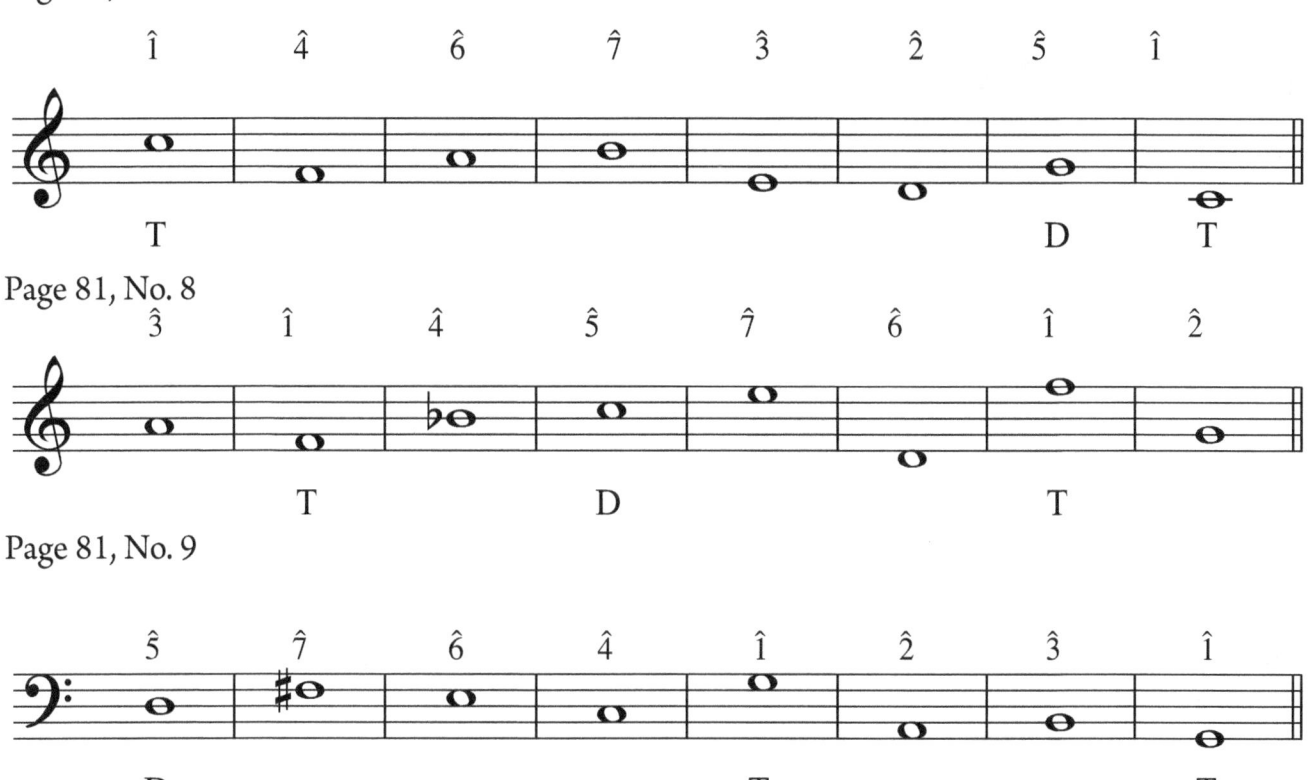

Page 81, No. 8

Page 81, No. 9

Page 83, No. 1

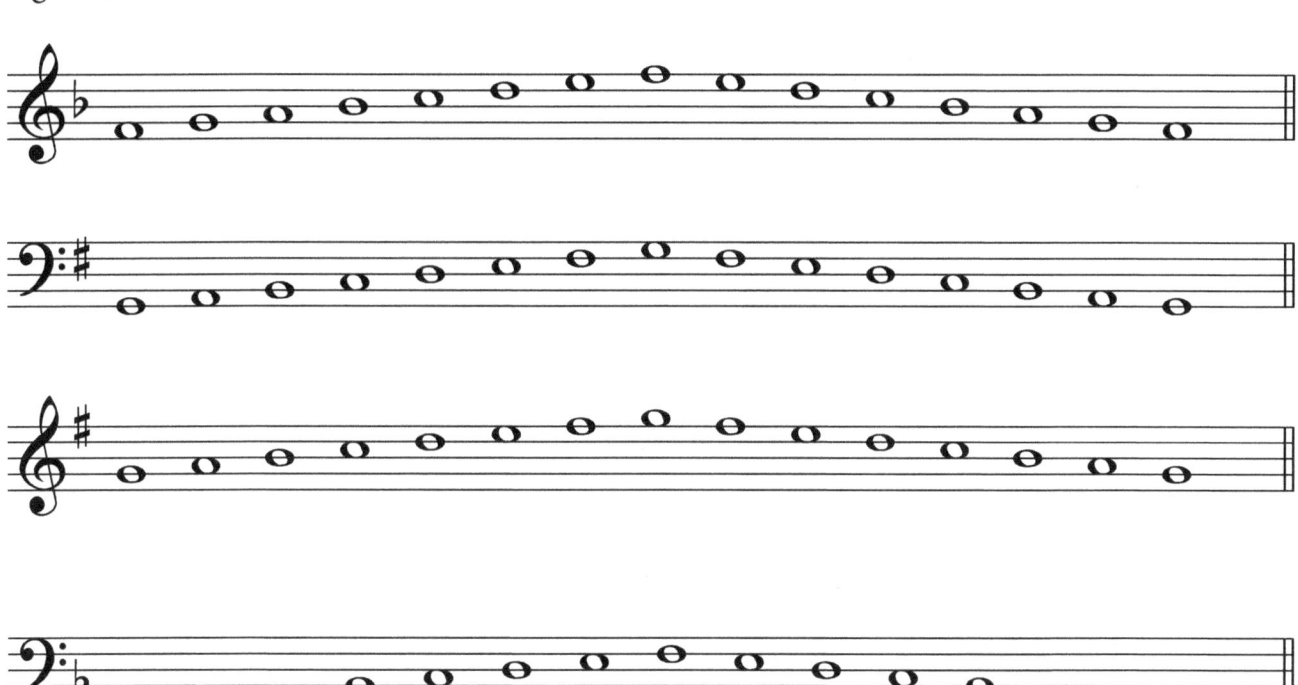

Page 84, No. 1

Page 85, No. 1
F major
G major
C major
F major

Page 86, No. 10

1 2 7 3 5 4

1 6 7 5 6

5 1 4 2 7

1 7 6 4 2

Page 87, No. 5

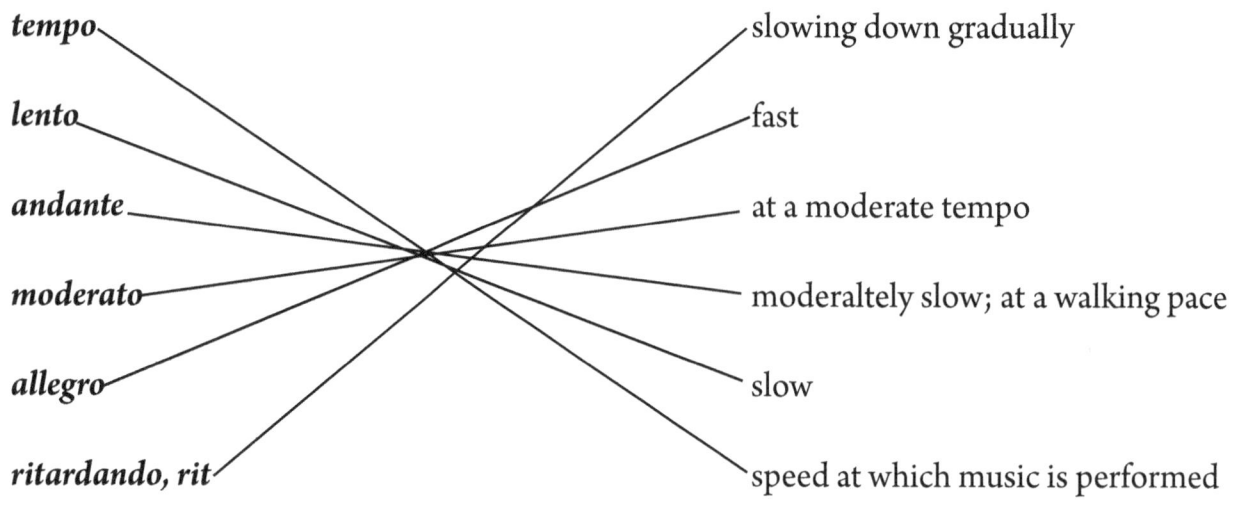

Page 88, No. 1

Page 89, No. 1

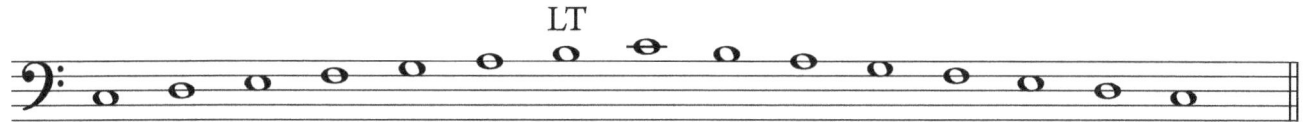

Page 90, No. 2

B♭ major

D major

F major

G major

C major

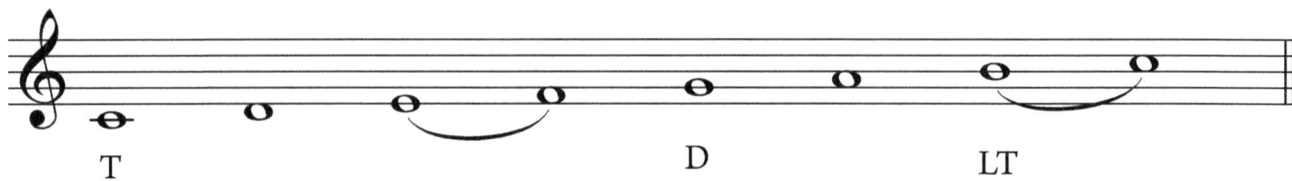

Page 91, No. 3

C major   B♭ major   D major   G major   F major

Page 91, No. 4

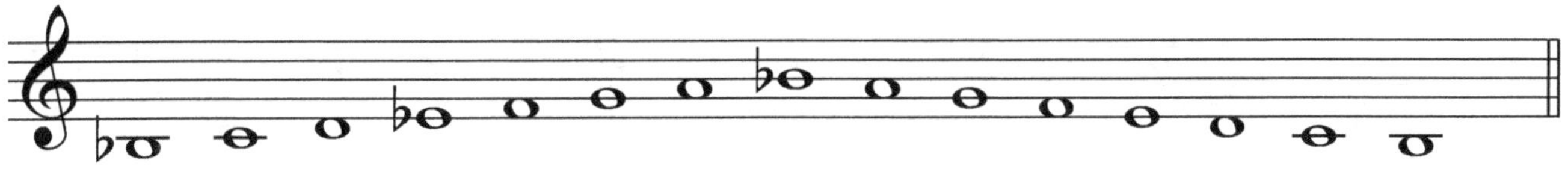

Bb major

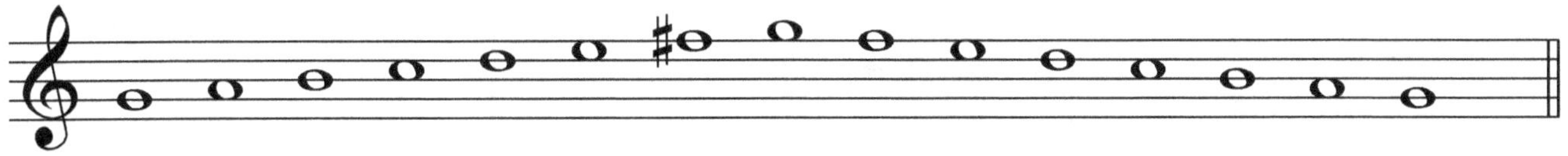

G major

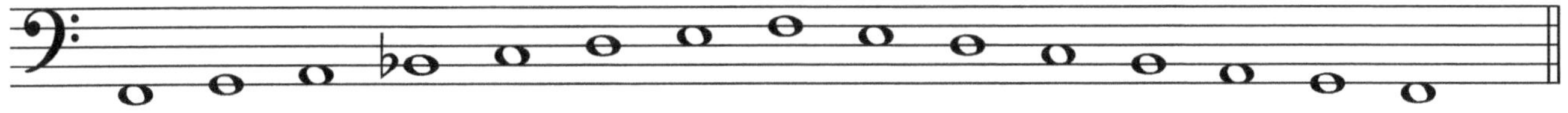

F major

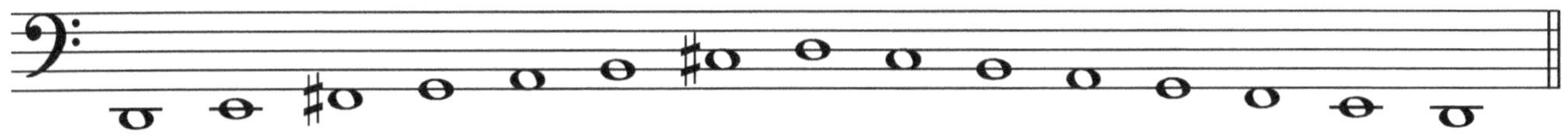

D major

Page 92, No. 5

E
D
Eb
D
B

Page 93, No. 6

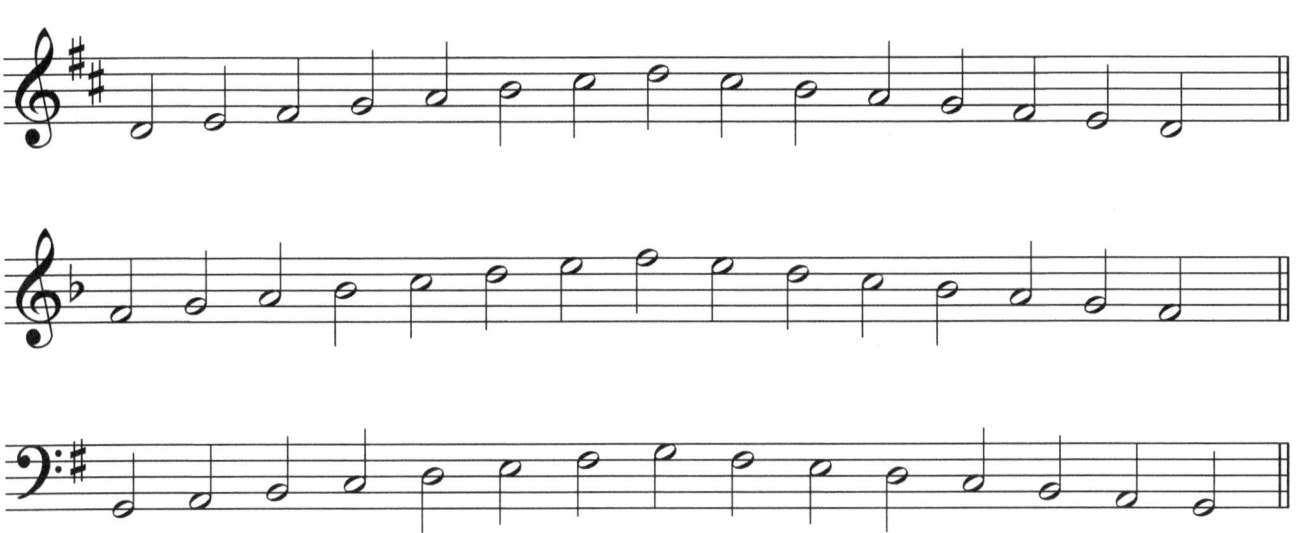

Page 95, No. 1

Page 97, No. 1

A minor

E minor

D minor

Page 97, No. 2

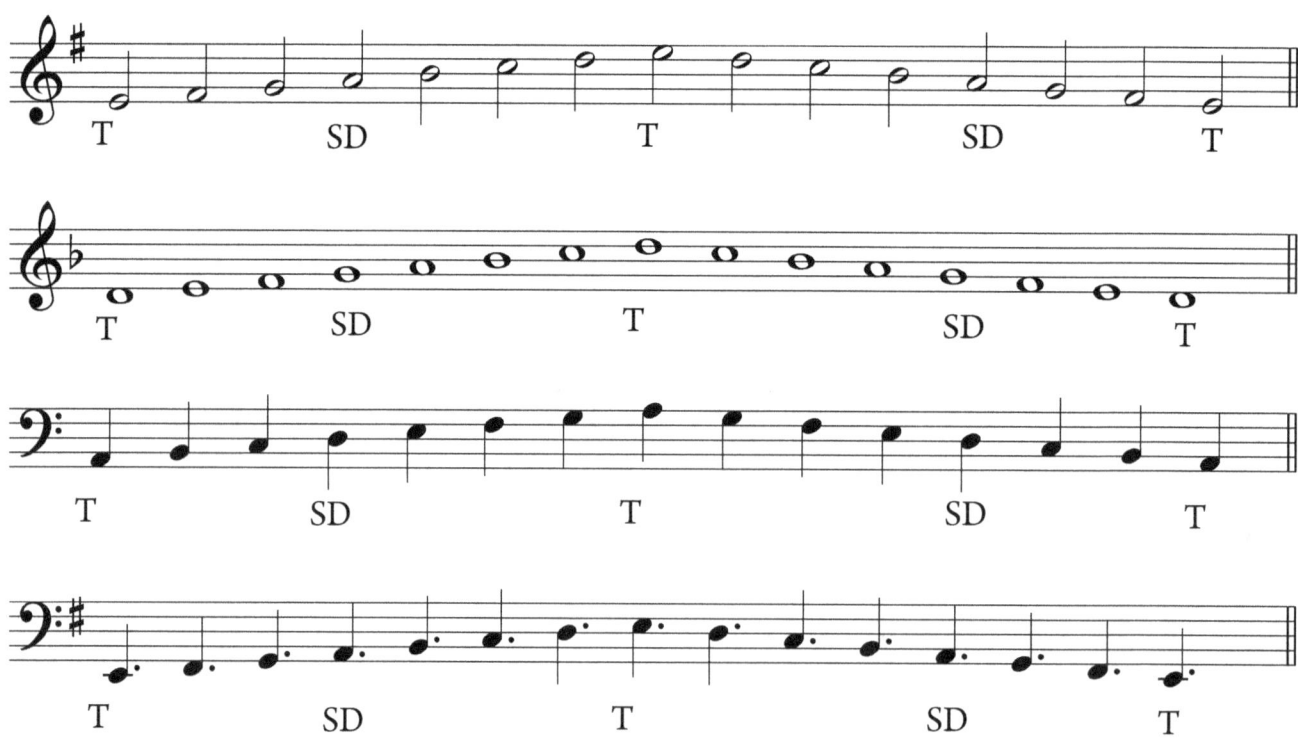

Page 99, No. 1

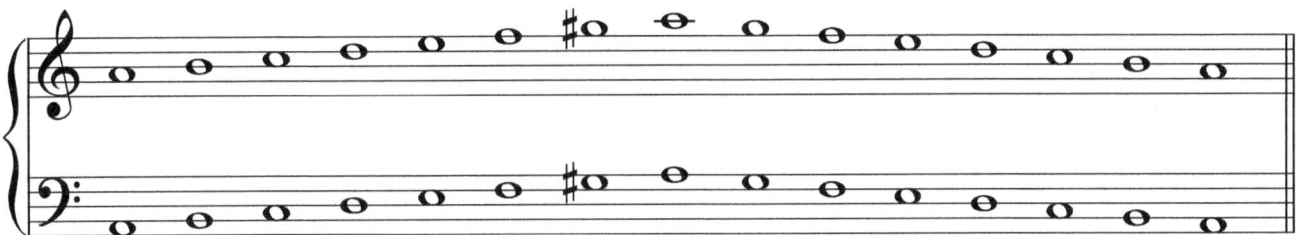

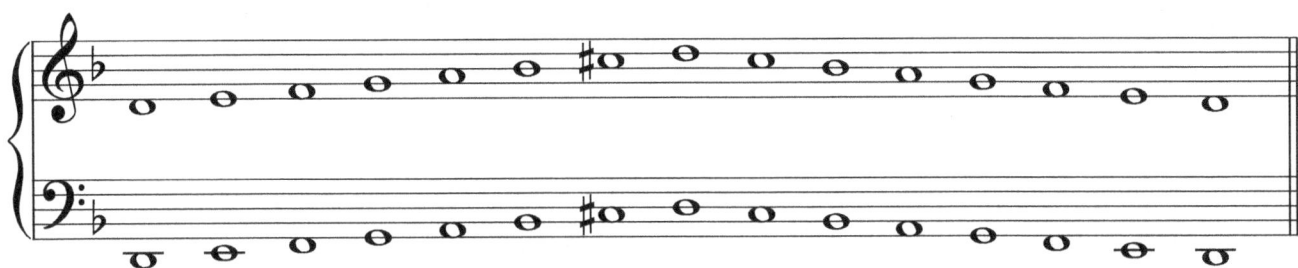

Page 100, No. 2

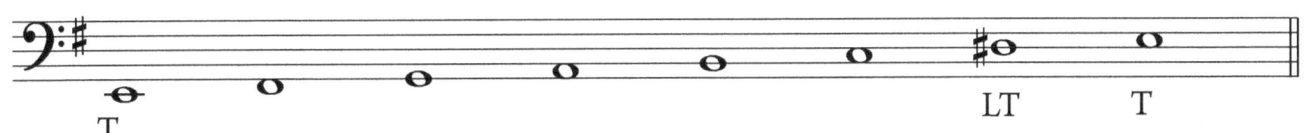

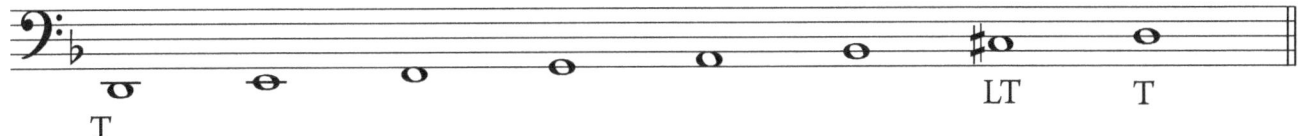

Page 101, No. 3

Page 103, No. 1

    D major **B minor**   B minor **D major**

    E minor **G major**   A minor **C major**

    C major **A minor**   G major **E minor**

    F major **D minor**   D minor **F major**

Page 103, No. 2

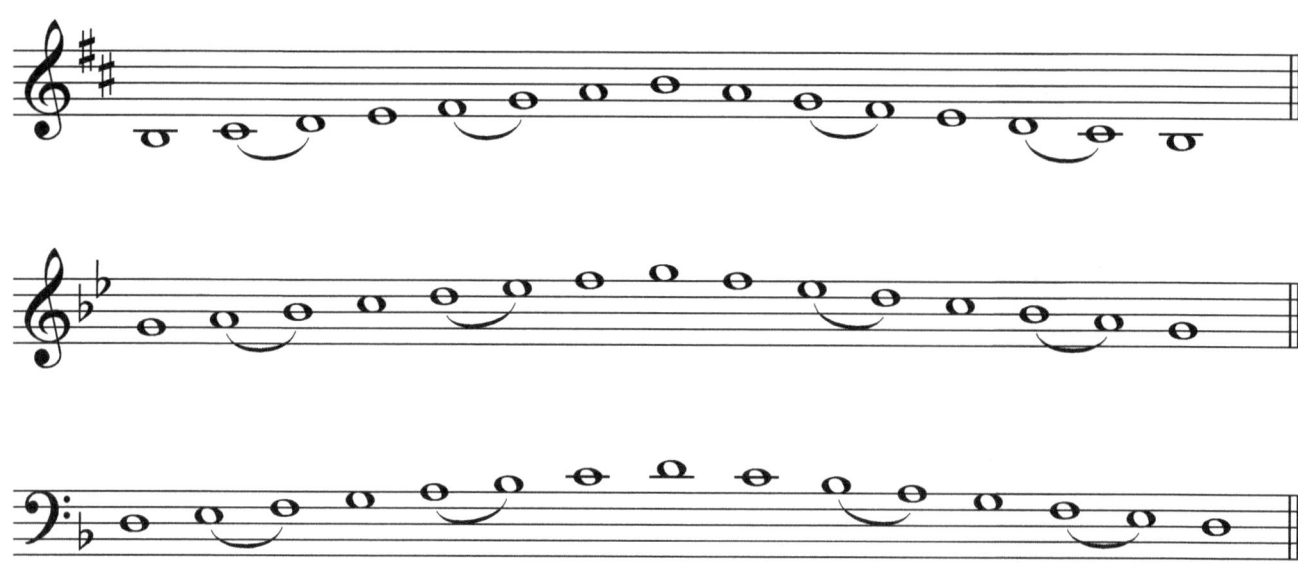

Page 105, No. 1

B minor

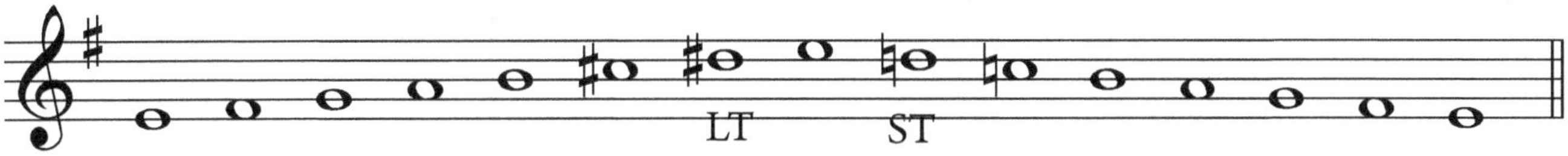

E minor

D minor

A minor

G minor

Page 106, No. 2

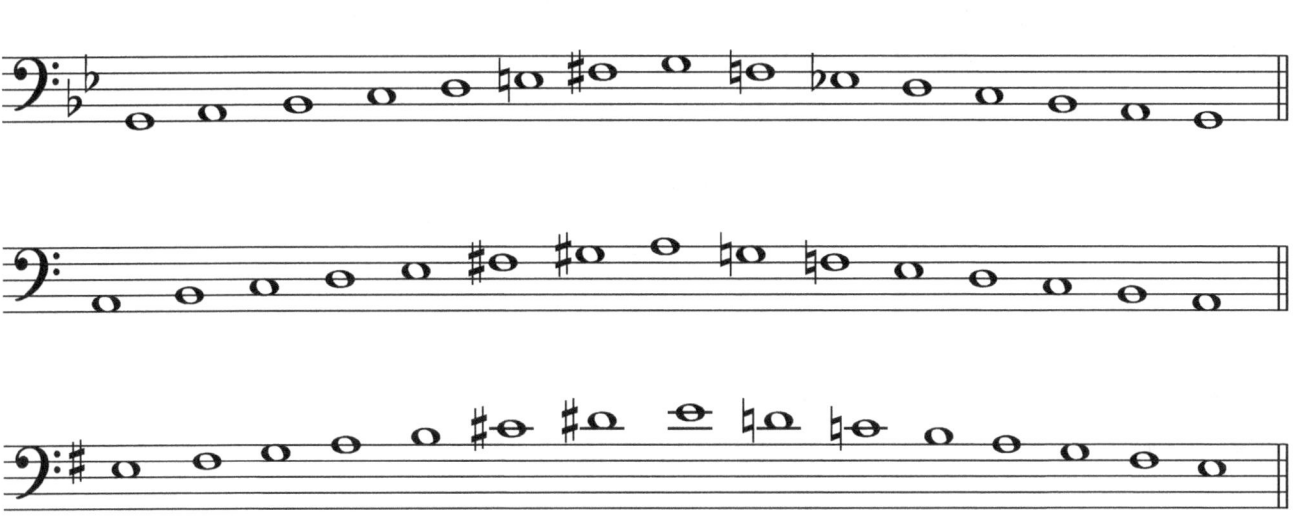

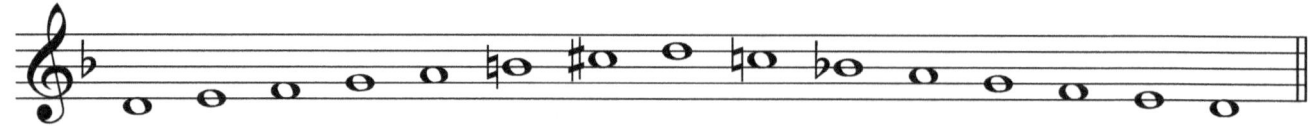

Page 107, No. 3

A harmonic minor

G natural minor

E melodic minor

D harmonic minor

B melodic minor

G melodic minor

Page 108, No. 4

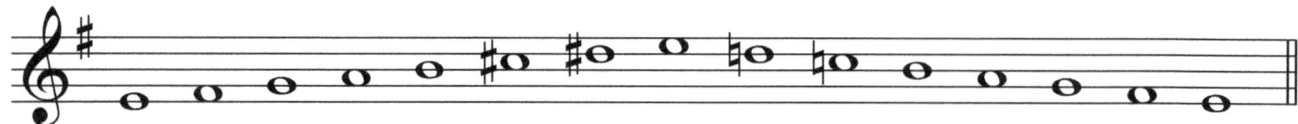

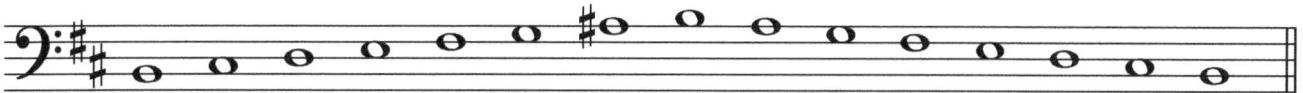

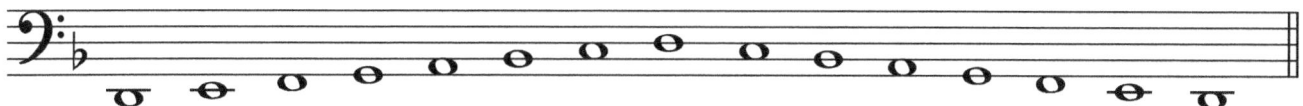

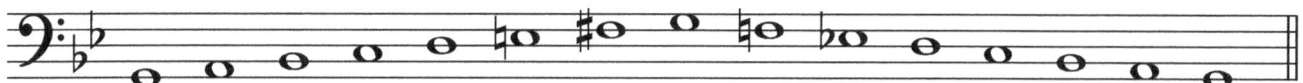

Page 109, No. 1

5 3 8 2 1 6

7 6 4 2 5 4

Page 110, No. 1

Page 111, No. 2

Page 111, No. 3

Page 111, No. 4

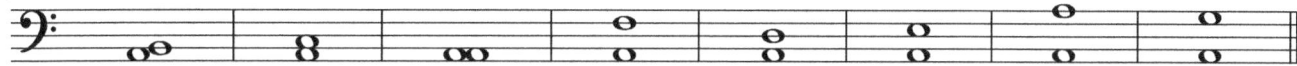

Page 111, No. 5

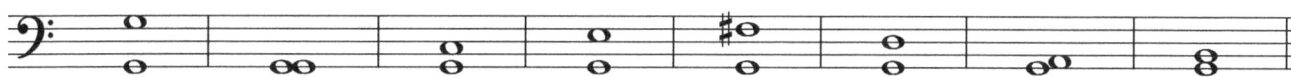

Page 114, No. 1

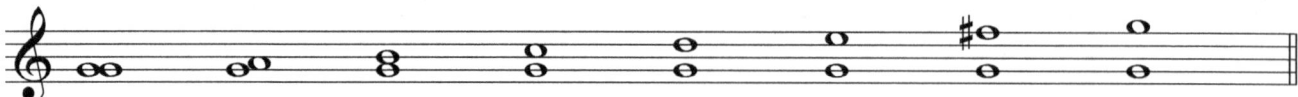

Page 114, No. 2

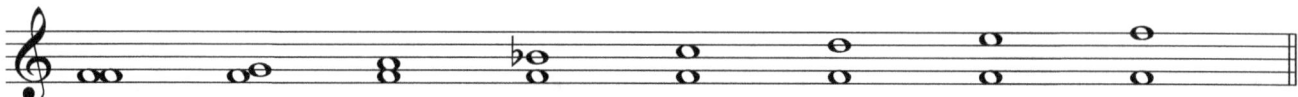

Page 114, No. 3

maj 6   per 4   maj 7   per 8   maj 2   per 4

maj 7   maj 3   per 4   per 5   per 8   per 1

Page 115, No. 4

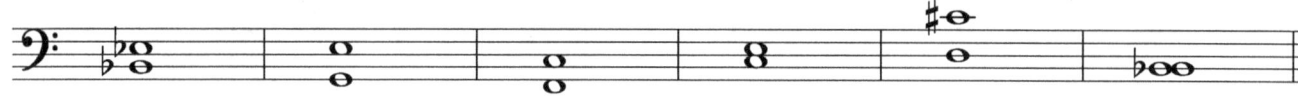

Page 115, No. 5

Page 116, No. 1

Page 116, No. 2

min 3   min 3   maj 3   min 3   maj 3
maj 3   min 3   maj 3   maj 3   min 3

Page 117, No. 3

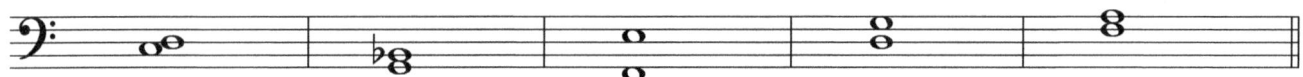

Page 117, No. 4

min 3   per 5   maj 2   maj 7   per 5
maj 3   min 3   per 8   maj 6   maj 7
min 3   per 4   maj 7   min 3   maj 6

Page 120, No. 1

Root:	C	Root:	F	Root:	G	Root:	A
Third:	E	Third:	A	Third:	B	Third:	C
Fifth:	G	Fifth:	C	Fifth:	D	Fifth:	E

Page 121, No. 2

F major	G major	C major	C major
F major	G major	G major	F major
A minor	C major	F major	G major
A minor	G major	F major	C major

Page 121, No. 3

Page 122, No. 4

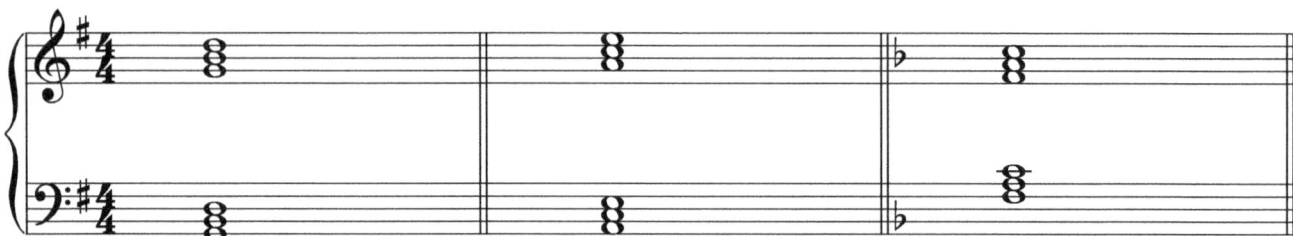

Page 122, No. 5

Triad	Root	3rd	5th
F major	F	A	C
G major	G	B	D
C major	C	E	G
A minor	A	C	E

Page 122, No. 6

key: G major

key: C major

key: F major

Page 125, No. 1

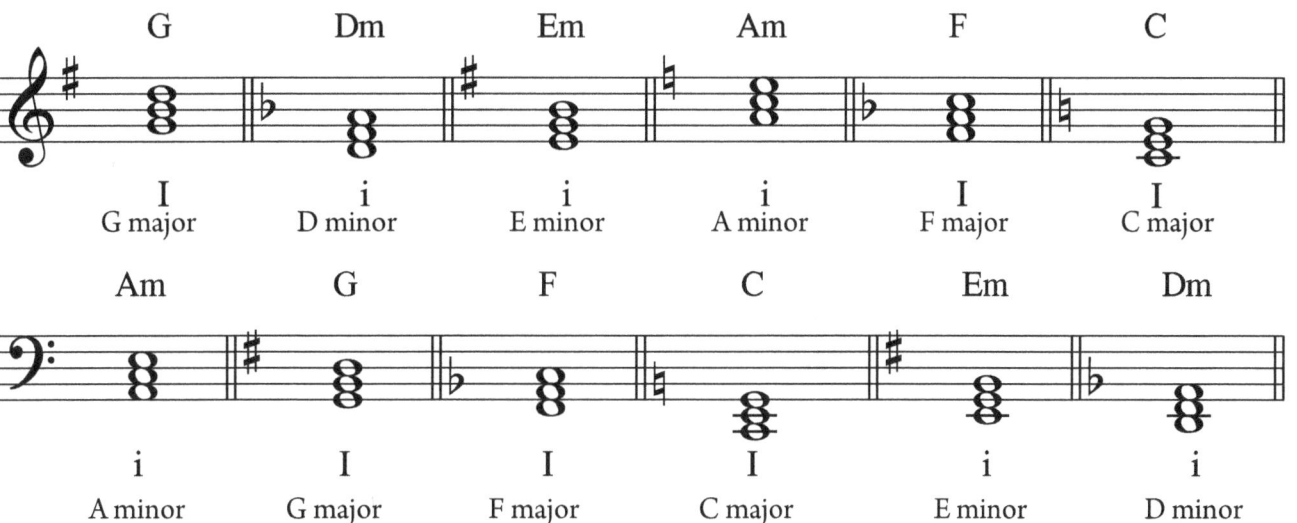

Page 125, No. 2 (naturals are optional, but not necessary after double bar)

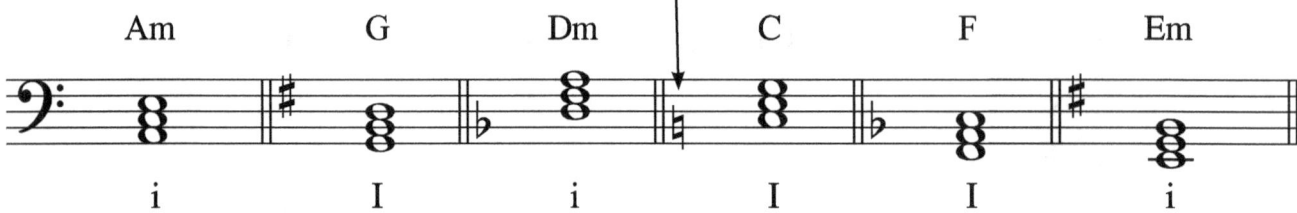

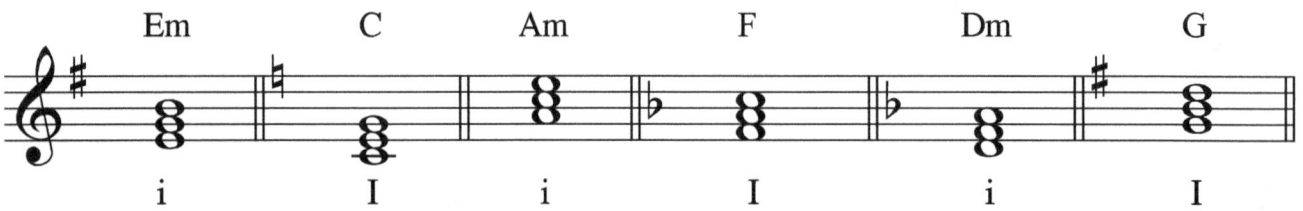

Page 126, No. 3

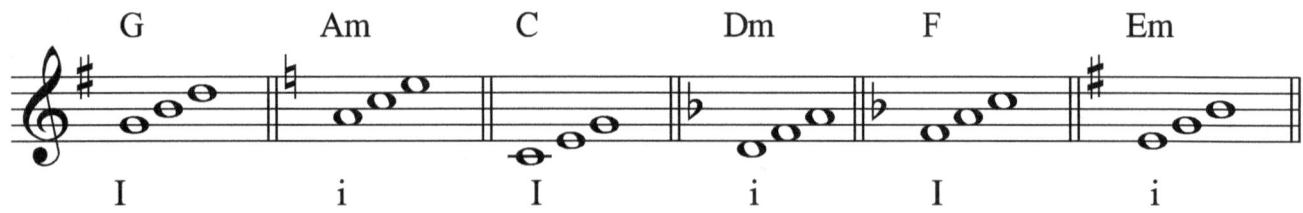

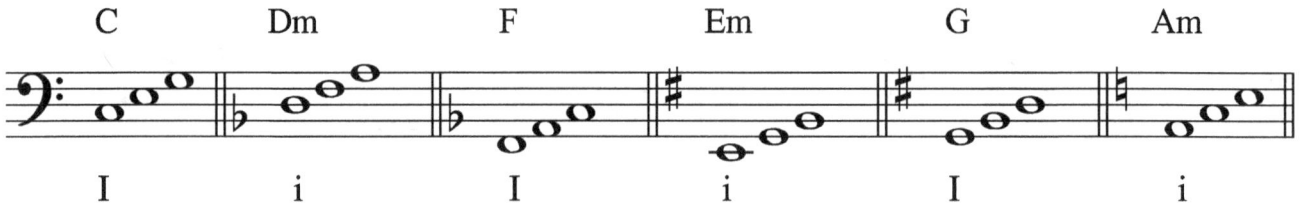

Page 126, No. 4

chord symbol:	**C**	chord symbol:	**Dm**	chord symbol:	**G**
key:	**C major**	key:	**D minor**	key:	**G major**
root:	**C**	root:	**D**	root:	**G**
3rd:	**E**	3rd:	**F**	3rd:	**B**
5th:	**G**	5th:	**A**	5th:	**D**

chord symbol:	**Em**	chord symbol:	**Am**	chord symbol:	**F**
key:	**E minor**	key:	**A minor**	key:	**F major**
root:	**E**	root:	**A**	root:	**F**
3rd:	**G**	3rd:	**C**	3rd:	**A**
5th:	**B**	5th:	**E**	5th:	**C**

Page 128, No. 1

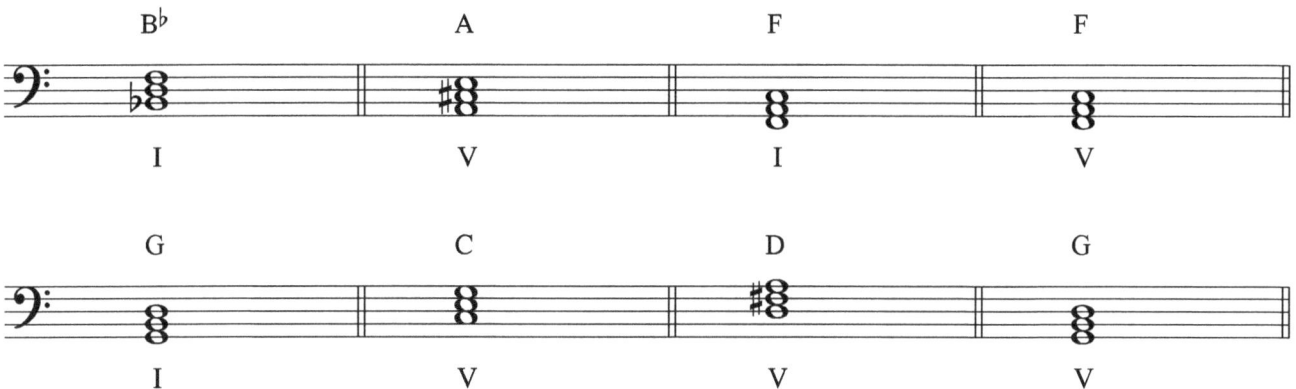

Page 129, No. 2

Page 130, No. 1

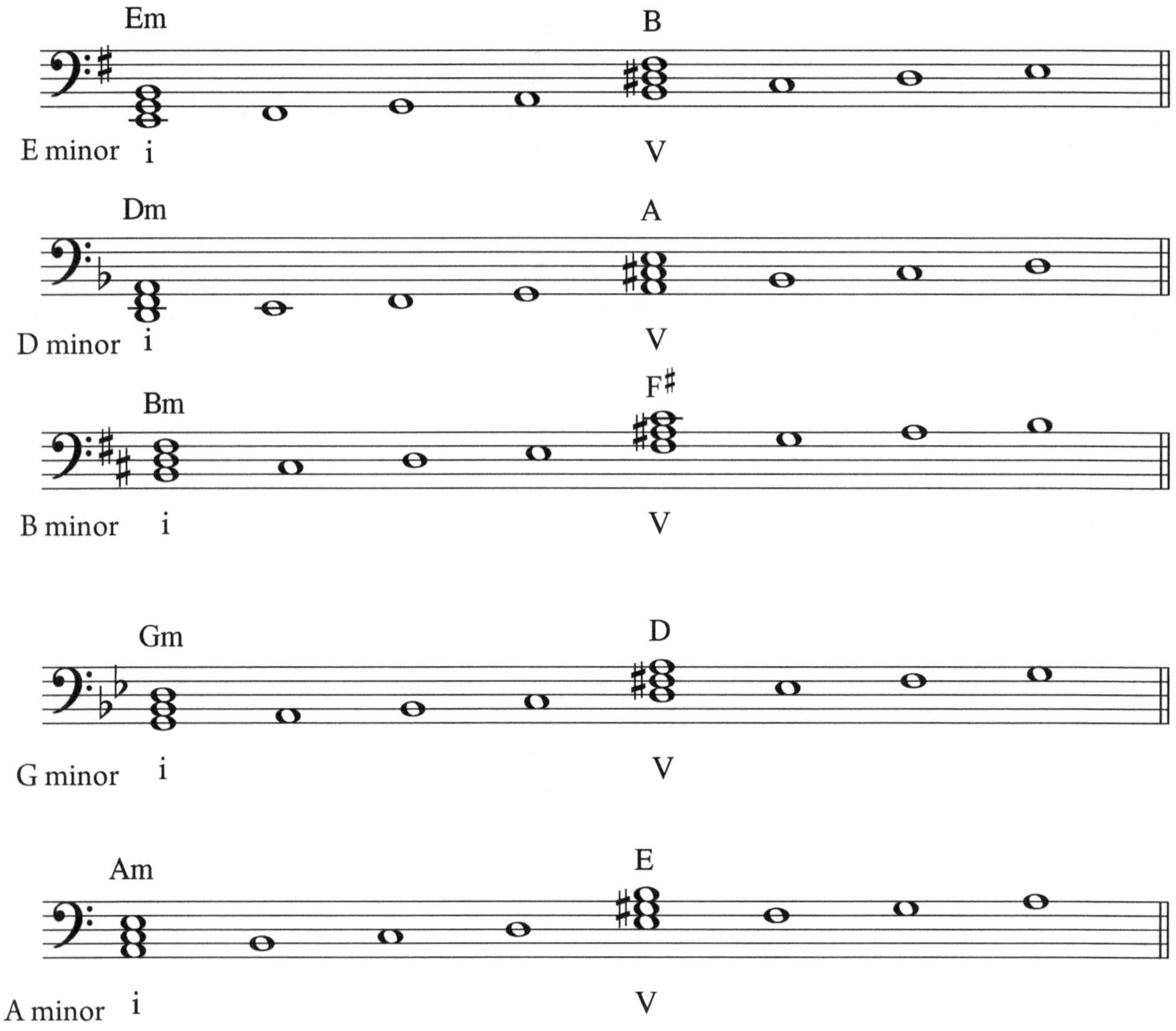

Page 131, No. 2

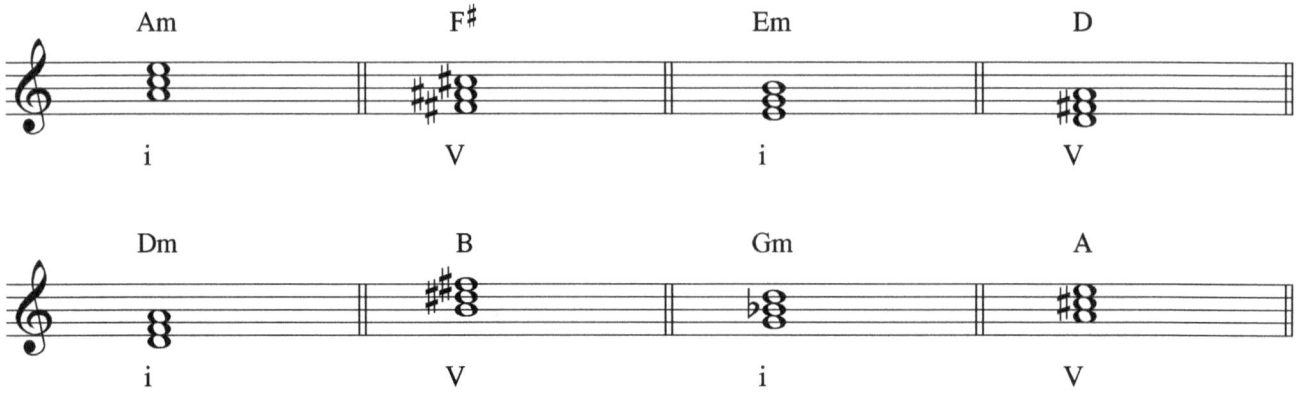

Page 131, No. 3

tonic	dominant	tonic	tonic
A minor i	D minor V	B minor i	E minor i

dominant	dominant	dominant	dominant
G minor V	E minor V	A minor V	B minor V

Page 133, No. 1

key: F major

key: C major

Page 135, No. 1 (other options are possible)

Page 135, No. 2 (other options are possible)

Page 135, No. 3

Page 137, No. 1

F major	$\hat{2}$	unstable
C major	$\hat{1}$	stable
G major	$\hat{3}$	stable

Page 138, No. 1

F major

C major

G major

Page 140, No. 1 (other options are possible)

Page 140, No. 2 (other options are possible)

Page 140, No. 3 (other options are possible)

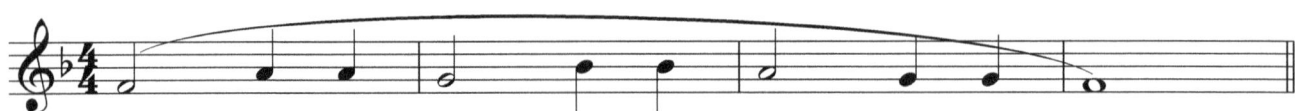

Page 141, No. 4 (other options are possible)

Page 141, No. 5 (other options are possible)

Page 141, No. 6

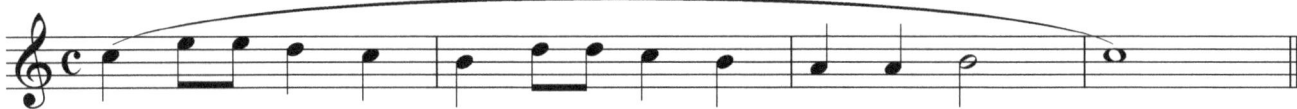

Page 144, No. 1 (other options are possible)

Page 144, No. 2 (other options are possible)

Page 144, No. 3 (other options are possible)

Page 145, No. 4 (other options are possible)

Page 145, No. 5 (other options are possible)

Page 146, No. 1

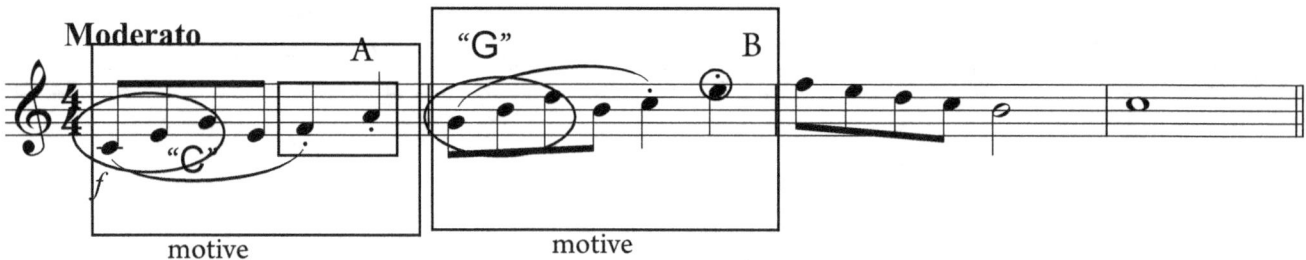

a. Add the correct time signature directly on the music.

b. Name the key of this piece. C major

c. Name the interval at A. 3rd

d. Find and circle a C major triad. Label it "C."

e. Find and circle a G major triad. Label it "G."

f. Define **Moderato**. at a moderate speed

g. Name and define the sign at letter B. staccato, play short and detached

h. Find a motive and draw a square around each time it occurs.

i. How many slurs are in this piece? 2

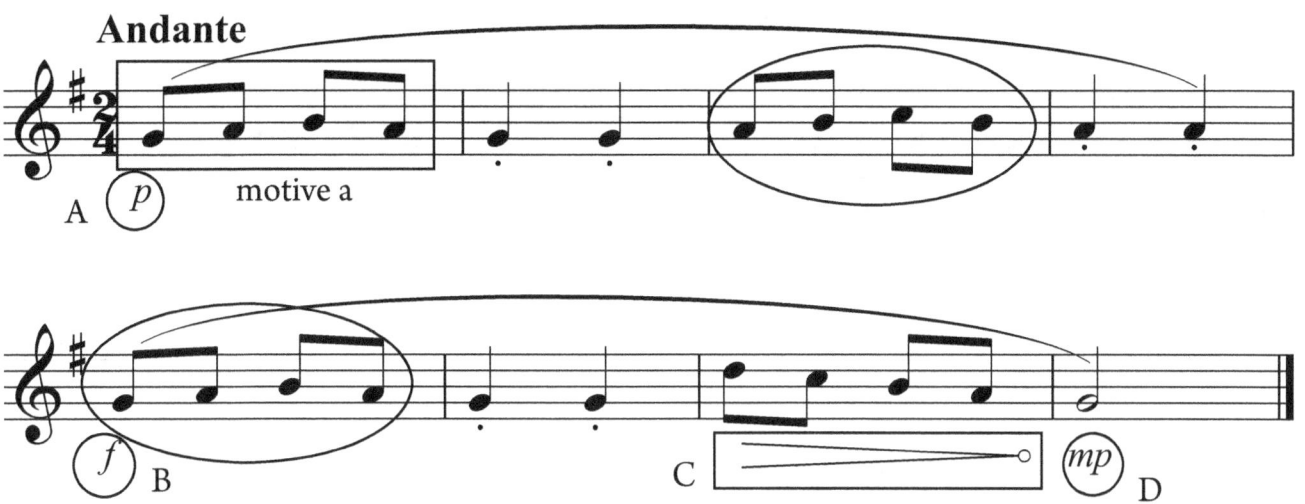

a. Add the correct time signature directly on the music.

b. Name the key of this piece. G major

c. Circle each time motive "a" appears in this piece.

d. How many phrases are in this piece? 2.

e. On which scale degree does phrase two end? $\hat{1}$

f. Define **Andante**. moderately slow, at a walking pace

g. Name and define the sign at letter A. piano, play soft

h. Name and define the sign at letter B. forte, play loud

i. Name and define the sign at letter C. decrescendo, becoming softer

j. Name and define the sign at letter D. mezzo piano, play moderately soft

Bagatelle

Anton Diabelli
(1781 - 1858)

a. What is the title of this piece? Bagatelle

b. Who is the composer? Anton Diabelli

c. Name the key of this piece G major

d. Add the time signature directly on the music.

e. How many phrases are in this piece? 1.

f. On which scale degree does the melody this piece begin? $\hat{5}$

g. Define **Allegro**. fast

h. Name the interval at A. 3rd

i. Name the interval at B. 4th

j. This piece is played:

☑ loud   ☐ soft

Page 149, No. 1

a. Add the correct time signature directly on the music.

b. Name the key of this piece. **F major**

c. Circle a complete F major scale in this piece.

d. Draw a phrase mark over the phrase.

e. On which scale degree does this phrase end? **1̂**

f. Is this a stable degree? **yes**

g. Define *Allegro*. **fast**

h. Explain the sign at letter A. **fortissimo, very loud**

i. Explain the sign at letter B. **fermata, pause**

j. Label all the leading tones **LT.**

Page 150

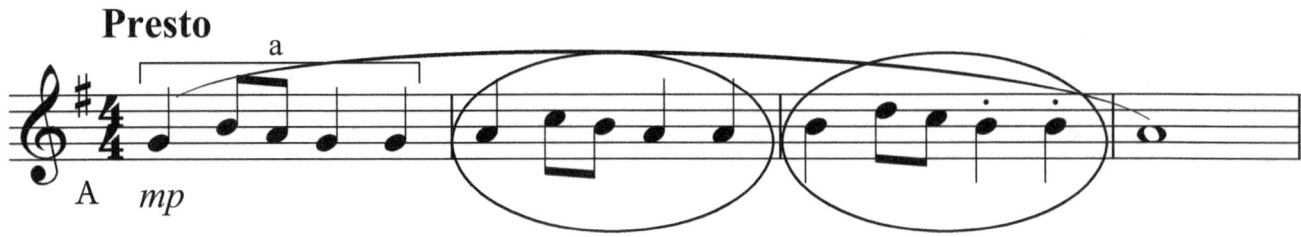

a. Add the correct time signature directly on the music.

b. Name the key of this piece. **G major**

c. Circle each time motive "a" appears in this piece.

d. There are two phrases. Draw a phrase mark over each phrase.

e. On which scale degree does this phrase one end? $\hat{2}$

f. Is this a stable degree? **no**

g. Define *Presto*. **very fast**

h. Explain the sign at letter A. **mezzo piano, moderately soft**

i. Explain the sign at letter B. **pianissimo, very soft**

j. Name and define the sign at letter C. **staccato, play short and detached**

Allegro in C

Alexander Reinagle
(1756 - 1809)

a. Give the title of this piece. **Allegro in C**

b. Add the correct time signature directly on the music.

c. Name the key of this piece. **C major**

d. Name the composer of this piece. **Alexander Reinagle**

e. When did he live? **1756- 1809**

f. There are two phrases. Draw a phrase mark over each phrase.

g. On which scale degree does phrase two end? **1̂**

h. Is this a stable degree? **yes**

i. Define *Molto allegro*. **Very fast**

j. Name and define the sign at A. **forte, loud**

k. Name the interval at B. **3rd**

Page 153-154, No. 1

Page 155

Allegro

Alexander Reinagle
(1756 - 1809)

a. Add the correct time signature directly on the music.

b. Name the key of this piece. **C major**

c. Name the composer of this piece. **Alexander Reinagle**

d. Draw a phrase mark over each phrase.

e. Label the phrases according to the form (a, a¹, b)

f. These two phrases form a: ☑ contrasting period ☐ parallel period

g. Does the second phrase end on a stable or unstable degree? **stable**

h. Define *Allegro*. **fast**

i. How are measure 1 and 2 similar to 5 and 6? **The rhythm is the same.**

i. Locate and circle a half step in this piece.

Page 156

Carefree

Daniel Gottlob Turk
((1756 - 1813))

a. Add the correct time signature directly on the music.

b. Name the key of this piece. **G major**

c. Name the composer of this piece. **Daniel Gottlob Turk**

d. Draw a phrase mark over each phrase.

e. Label the phrases according to the form (a, a¹, b)

f. These two phrases form a: ☐ contrasting period   ☑ parallel period

g. Does the second phrase end on a stable or unstable degree? **stable**

h. Define *Moderato*. **at a moderate speed**

i. Find and circle one accidental in this piece.

j. Name the interval at letter A. **maj 2**

k. Name the interval at letter B. **per 1**

54

Page 157

Bagatelle

Anton Diabelli

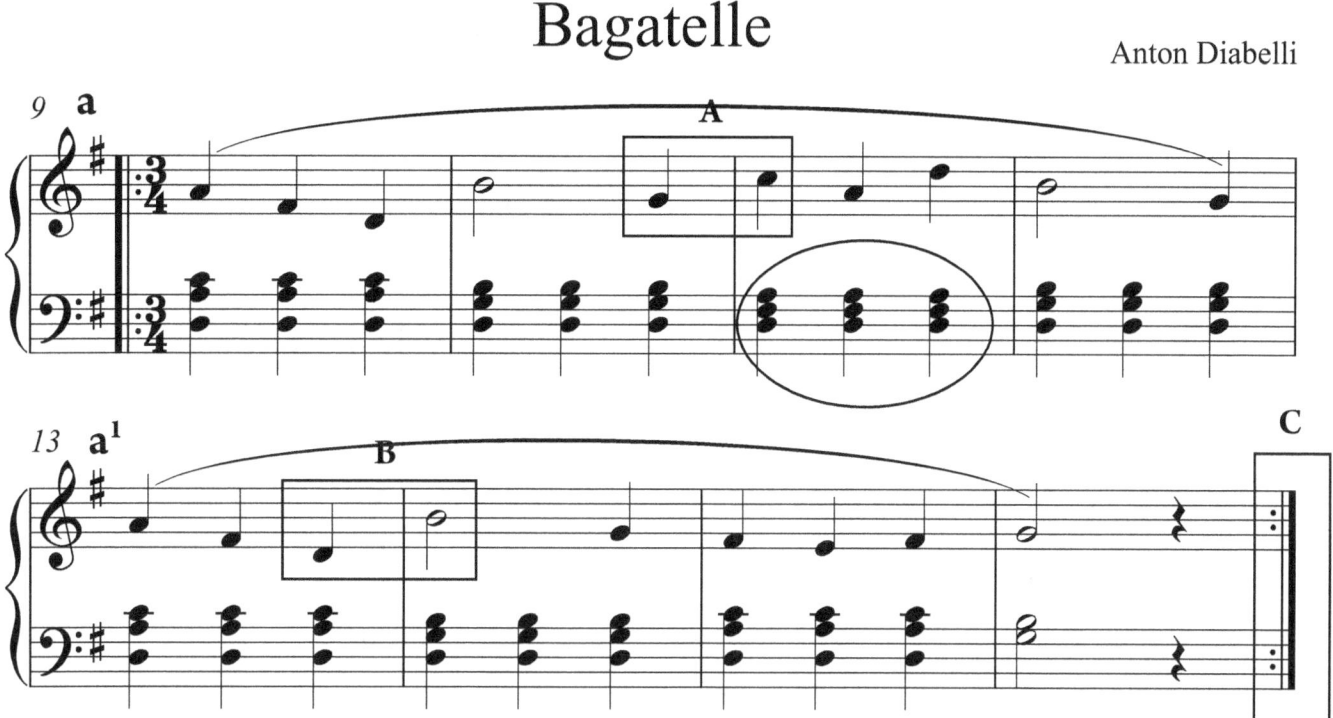

a. Add the correct time signature directly on the music.

b. Name the key of this piece. **G major**

c. Name the composer of this piece. **Anton Diabelli**

d. Draw a phrase mark over each phrase.

e. Label the phrases according to the form (a, a¹, b)

f. Does the second phrase end on a stable or unstable degree? **stable**

g. Find and circle one dominant triad in this piece.

h. Name the interval at letter A. **per 4**

i. Name the interval at letter B. **maj 6**

j. Explain the sign at letter C. **Repeat sign. Repeat the music between the repeat signs.**

k. On what measure does this piece begin? **9**

Page 161

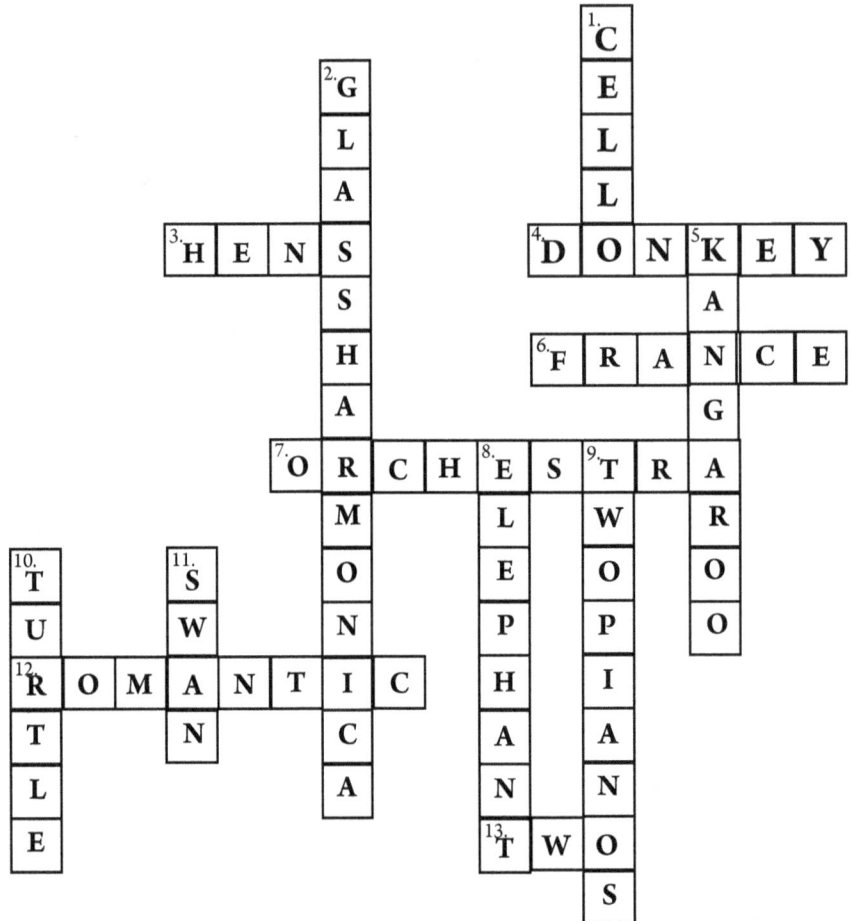

Page 162

a. ☑Conductor
b. ☑Maracas
c. ☑French Horn
d. ☑France
e. ☑3
f. ☑2 pianos
g. ☑Wolf
h. ☑Glass Harmonic
i. ☑Cello
j. ☑Program Music

Page 165

1. Where was Prokofiev born? **Russia**
2. At what age did Prokofiev begin composing? **five**
3. In what musical era did he compose? **Modern**
4. Peter and the Wolf is written for narrator and **orchestra**
5. What type of music is Peter and the Wolf? **Program**
6. Name 4 animals in Peter and the Wolf. **Wolf, duck, cat, bird**
7. What instruments are used to portray Peter? **strings**
8. What instrument is used to portray the grandfather? **bassooon**
9. What instument is used to portray the duck? **oboe**

Page 168

a. Austria
b. His father
c. classical
d. french horn
e. movements
f. rondo
g. piano
h. 12
i. theme
j. Twinkle Twinkle, Baa Baa Black Sheep, Alphabet Song

Page 174

a) Baroque
b) 1685-1750
c) Germany
d) Two books of keyboard music that J.S. Bach gave to his wife Anna Magdalena
e) J.S. Bach, Johann Christian Bach, C.P.E. Bach, Christian Petzold, Francois Couperin
f) dances, arias, chorales
g) harpsichord
h) keyboard
i) France
j) 3/4
k) France
l) yes
m) Allegro, Vivace, Presto
n) three
o) the end

www.ingramcontent.com/pod-product-compliance
Lightning Source LLC
Chambersburg PA
CBHW081733100526
44591CB00016B/2596